"Turn Your Ideas Into A Coffee Business Now"

BUILD A BUSINESS

From The Small Steps

Dragan Ristic

"Turn Your Ideas Into A Coffee Business Now"

BUILD A BUSINESS

From The Small Steps

Copyright © 2023 by Dragan Ristic

TABLE OF CONTENTS

BOOK INTRODUCTION

Starting and running a coffee business can be a rewarding and challenging project, but with the right planning and execution, it can be a successful and fulfilling journey. In this book, we provide a comprehensive guide to setting up and running a coffee business, covering a variety of topics that are essential for coffee business owners to consider.

From market research and business planning to financing options and marketing strategies, this book covers the key factors that can impact the success of a coffee business.

We also dive into the challenges and opportunities that coffee businesses may face and provide expert advice on how to overcome these challenges and seize opportunities.

Whether you are a coffee enthusiast looking to start your own coffee shop or coffee roastery, or an experienced business owner looking to expand your coffee business, this book provides valuable insights and practical guidance to help you succeed. With its step-by-step approach and expert advice, this book is an essential resource for anyone looking to set up and run a successful coffee business.

Book is designed systematically by chapters where each of the chapters will have introduction part, listed points part, and conclusion part. By doing this author of the book was aiming for uniformity and consistency for easier following and absorbing professional and complex book content.

It's written on the way that you will give you feeling of sitting next to the real consultant and writing down necessary steps to consider before and during business setup and all to make sure to avoid mistakes that could potentially cost a lot after business start running.

BOOK OVERVIEW

Chapter 1: Introduction to the Coffee Industry:
Overview of the coffee industry, including current trends and market conditions.
Commercial and retail coffee.
Coffee as a commodity.
Coffee supply chain.
Market trends and statistics in the coffee industry.
Key players in the coffee industry.
Global and regional coffee markets
Environmental and social factors in the coffee industry.
Challenges facing the coffee industry.
Opportunities in the coffee industry.

Chapter 2: Market Research:
Importance of market research in starting a coffee business.
Steps for conducting market research, including:
Defining your target market, analyzing the competition, analyze market demand and to gather market intelligence.
Tips for collecting and analyzing market data including:
Understanding the Coffee Industry, Conducting Market Research, SWOT Analysis, Key Findings.

Chapter 3: Business Planning:
Importance of creating a business plan before starting a coffee business.
Steps for creating a business plan, including defining your business vision and mission, conducting a SWOT analysis, and

creating a marketing plan.
Tips for creating a financial plan, including forecasting revenue and expenses, and developing a budget.

Chapter 4: Choosing a Business Structure:
Overview of different business structures, including sole proprietorships, partnerships, LLCs, and corporations.
Pros and cons of each business structure.
Factors to consider when choosing a business structure.

Chapter 5: Financing Options:
Overview of different financing options, including loans, grants, and crowdfunding.
Pros and cons of each financing option.
Tips for securing financing for your coffee business.

Chapter 6: Setting Up the Physical Space:
Overview of the steps for setting up the physical space for a coffee shop or coffee roastery.
Steps for choosing a location, including evaluating the location, negotiating a lease, and obtaining necessary permits and licenses.
Steps for setting up the physical space, including designing the interior, purchasing equipment, and installing utilities.

Chapter 7: Staffing and Training:
Importance of staffing and training for a coffee business.
Steps for hiring and training employees, including recruiting and interviewing candidates, and providing on-the-job training.
Tips for developing a comprehensive training program for employees.

Chapter 8: Marketing and Promotion:

Importance of marketing and promotion for a coffee business. Steps for creating a marketing plan, including defining your target market, determining your marketing budget, and selecting appropriate marketing channels.

Tips for developing and implementing effective marketing strategies, including social media marketing, email marketing, and event marketing.

Chapter 9: Challenges and Opportunities:

Overview of common challenges faced by coffee businesses, including competition, rising costs, and changing consumer preferences.

Steps for identifying and overcoming challenges, including developing effective marketing strategies and improving operational efficiency.

Overview of opportunities for growth and expansion, including expanding your product line and entering new markets.

Chapter 10: Conclusion:

Summary of key takeaways from the book

Final thoughts and recommendations for starting and running a successful coffee business.

WELCOME

To the professional world of Coffee. If you are new in hospitality industry or new in the coffee industry, I advise you to start slowly with reading the content and to give yourself a time to soak everything slowly otherwise it might become overwhelming to absorb all the content. If you are already experienced in the hospitality industry in generally and have decent experience in the coffee industry you will be able easier to absorb book content. Whichever group of those two is yours welcome again, relax and let's start slowly this journey.

CHAPTER 1

INTRODUCTION TO COFFEE INDUSTRY

In this chapter, you will be introduced to the coffee industry and its growth over the years. You will learn about the different segments of the industry, such as specialty coffee, commercial coffee, and retail coffee. You will also learn about the importance of coffee as a beverage and how it has become a staple drink for many people around the world. You will learn as well about the coffee industry and the various aspects that make up this complex and dynamic market. This includes an overview of the industry, a discussion of the different types of coffee, and a look at the coffee supply chain. You will also gain an understanding of the market trends and statistics in the coffee industry, the key players, and the global and regional coffee markets. The chapter will explore the environmental and social factors that are affecting the coffee industry, as well as the challenges and opportunities facing the industry. This chapter will be the longest and probably most complex of all the chapters and will provide you with a comprehensive understanding of the coffee industry and help to set the stage for the rest of the book which will be spited in smaller, uniformly organized chapters.

1.1 Overview of the Coffee Industry:

The coffee industry is a complex and dynamic market that has evolved over centuries, originating in the coffee-growing regions of Africa, and spreading to the rest of the world. Today, coffee is one of the most popular beverages in the world, enjoyed by millions of people every day.

There are two main species of coffee beans: Arabica and Robusta. Arabica is considered to be the higher quality of the two and is grown at higher altitudes and in more specific climates. Robusta, on the other hand, is grown at lower altitudes and is known for its stronger, more bitter flavor.

Coffee can be brewed in a variety of ways, including espresso, pour-over, French press, cezve/ibrik and more. The method used to brew coffee can greatly impact its taste and quality. Specialty coffee is a growing segment of the coffee industry and is defined as coffee that is grown and processed with care and attention to detail, resulting in a unique and high-quality flavor.

Specialty coffee shops and roasteries are becoming increasingly popular, as consumers seek out high-quality, sustainably sourced coffee. It is important to have a comprehensive understanding of the coffee industry, including as well and   commercial and retail aspects. The coffee industry encompasses the entire supply chain from coffee production, processing, packaging, and distribution to retail sales. In this chapter, we will delve into the coffee industry and provide a detailed overview of its various components, including the history of coffee, the current state of the industry, market trends, and the key players involved.

1.1.1 History of coffee:

The origin of coffee dates to the ancient kingdoms of Ethiopia, where it is believed to have been discovered by a goat herder Kaldi who noticed that his goats became more energetic after eating the berries from a certain bush. Over time, the use of coffee spread throughout the world, first to Yemen and then to Java, Indonesia. Today, coffee is one of the world's most widely consumed beverages and is grown in countries all around the world, from South America to Africa to Asia.

1.1.2 Current state of the industry:

The current state of the coffee industry is characterized by a highly competitive and dynamic market, with a growing demand for specialty and high-quality coffee. With the rise of specialty coffee shops, there has been a significant increase in the number of small and independent coffee roasters, each offering unique blends and flavors. The growth of the industry has also led to a rise in the number of coffee farmers, who are producing high-quality beans that are in high demand by coffee roasters and consumers alike.

1.1.3 Key Players in the Industry:

The coffee industry is made up of a wide range of players, from coffee farmers and processors to roasters and retailers. Some of the key players in the industry include large coffee companies such as Starbucks, Dunkin' Donuts, and Tim Hortons, as well as smaller, independent coffee shops and roasters.

1.1.4 The Specialty Coffee Market:

The specialty coffee market is a rapidly growing segment of the coffee industry, and is defined by its focus on high-quality, sustainably sourced, and ethically produced coffee.

The key drivers of the specialty coffee market include taste, quality, and sustainability, and these factors are shaping the future of the coffee industry.

Specialty coffee shops and roasteries offer a unique experience to customers, with a focus on craftsmanship, knowledge, and service.

These businesses often source their coffee directly from the farmers who grow it, allowing for a more transparent and sustainable supply chain.

1.1.5 Coffee Industry Trends and Forecast:

The coffee industry is constantly evolving, and it's important for coffee businesses to stay ahead of the trends and forecast.

Some of the current trends in the coffee industry include the rise of specialty coffee, the growth of sustainable and ethical coffee production, and the increasing popularity of coffee-based drinks such as cold brew and nitro coffee

The growth potential of the specialty coffee market is strong, but there are also challenges and opportunities that coffee businesses must consider.

Consumer preferences are changing, and there is a growing demand for high-quality, sustainably sourced, and ethically produced coffee.

Competition is also increasing, as more specialty coffee shops and roasteries opens. Additionally, the rising costs of coffee beans, labor, and other factors can impact the bottom line of coffee businesses. By staying ahead of the trends and forecasting in the coffee industry, coffee businesses can position themselves for success and ensure they are able to meet the evolving needs and demands of their customers.

1.1.6 Coffee Production and Supply Chain:

Coffee is produced in many countries around the world, with the top producing countries being Brazil, Vietnam, and Colombia. From the farm to the cup, coffee goes through a complex supply chain that involves many different actors, including growers, exporters, importers, roasters, and retailers. Understanding the coffee supply chain is critical to ensuring that you have a consistent and high-quality supply of coffee beans for your shop or roastery.

COFFEE PRODUCING COUNTRIES

- BRAZIL IS THE BIGGEST COFFEE EXPORTER WITH APROX. 60 MILION BAGS PER YEAR.

- BRAZIL = BIGGEST ARABICA EXPORTER

- VIETNAM = BIGGEST ROBUSTA EXPORTER

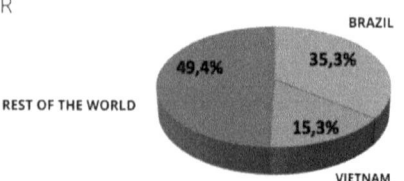

1.1.7 Market Size and Growth:

The global coffee market is growing at a fast pace, driven by increased demand for coffee, particularly specialty coffee. The market is expected to continue to grow in the coming years, creating opportunities for new entrants into the industry. Understanding the size and growth of the market will help you to identify the potential for your business and make informed decisions about your strategy.

GLOBAL COFFEE PRODUCTION

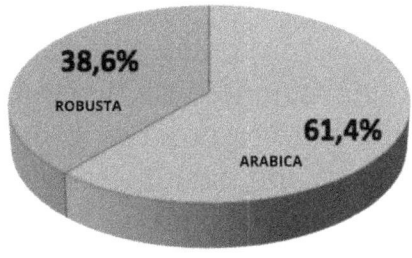

1.2 Commercial and Retail Coffee:

The commercial coffee industry refers to the production, distribution, and sale of coffee products for wholesale and business-to-business (B2B) purposes. This sector of the coffee industry is responsible for providing coffee to coffee shops, cafes, restaurants, and other commercial establishments.

The commercial coffee industry is a critical component of the overall coffee industry as it provides the bulk of the coffee used in cafes and other establishments.

There are various players in the commercial coffee industry, including coffee roasters, coffee wholesalers, and coffee importers.

Coffee roasters play a key role in the commercial coffee industry by sourcing commercial quality green coffee beans and roasting them to produce coffee that is sold to commercial market and customers who prefer such product which is by many parameters different from Specialty Coffee product.

Coffee wholesalers and importers are also important players in the commercial coffee industry as they help to distribute coffee to a wider range of customers, including both commercial and retail customers.

The commercial coffee industry is constantly evolving, with new trends emerging and old ones fading away.

One of the key trends in the commercial coffee industry is the focus on sustainable and ethically sourced coffee. As consumers become more concerned about the environmental impact of coffee production and the treatment of workers in the coffee industry, many coffee companies are looking to source coffee that is grown in a sustainable and ethical manner. This trend has led to an increased demand for specialty coffee, which is coffee that is grown in a specific region and has unique flavor characteristics.

Another trend in the commercial coffee industry is the use of technology to improve the efficiency and quality of the coffee-making process. For example, some coffee shops and cafes are now using automated espresso machines and other equipment that allow baristas to make coffee with greater precision and consistency. This technology is also helping to reduce waste in the coffee-making process, as baristas can make coffee that is consistent in flavor and quality.

Overall, the commercial coffee industry is a complex and dynamic sector of the coffee industry that is critical to the success of coffee shops, cafes, and other commercial establishments. Whether you are starting a coffee business or are a seasoned coffee professional, it is important to understand the trends and challenges in the commercial coffee industry to stay ahead of the competition and ensure long-term success.

Retail coffee refers to the sales and distribution of coffee products to consumers through various channels, such as coffee shops, supermarkets, and online platforms. The retail coffee industry has grown significantly in recent years, driven by increased consumer demand for high-quality, specialty coffee. Consumers are increasingly interested in the origin, quality, and sustainability of their coffee, and are willing to pay premium prices for coffee products that meet these criteria.

Coffee shops are the most visible face of the retail coffee industry, offering customers a place to enjoy coffee and socialize. Coffee shops are found in all sorts of locations, from city centers to rural areas, and offer a wide range of coffee products and services.

There are several different types of retail coffee establishments, each with its own unique offerings and target audience. Some of the most common types include:

- **Coffee shops:**

  Coffee shops are typically fast-paced, low-cost venues that serve a variety of coffee, tea, and snack options. They may also offer baked goods and other food items.

- **Cafes:**

  Cafes are typically more upscale than coffee shops and often feature a sit-down atmosphere. They may offer a more extensive menu that includes breakfast and lunch items, as well as specialty coffee and tea beverages.

- **Specialty coffee shops:**

  Specialty coffee shops focus on high-quality coffee and

tea, offering a wide selection of beans, blends, and roasts. They may also offer baked goods, pastries, and other food items.

The retail coffee industry is highly competitive, with many established players and new entrants vying for market share. To succeed, retail coffee establishments must differentiate themselves from the competition through factors such as location, quality, customer service, and price. Additionally, they must stay ahead of trends and adapt to changes in consumer preferences and behavior in order to remain relevant and competitive.

1.3 Coffee as a commodity:

The coffee industry is a complex and multifaceted industry that encompasses a wide range of participants, from coffee farmers and processors to roasters, retailers, and consumers. One of the key aspects of this industry is coffee as a commodity. In this chapter, you will learn about what coffee as a commodity is, how it is traded, and its role in the overall coffee industry.

1.3.1 What is Coffee as a Commodity?

Coffee is a commodity that is traded on various exchanges around the world. Commodities are raw materials or primary products that are bought and sold based on their market value. Coffee is considered a commodity because it is a standardized product that is grown in many different regions, with a large global supply, and is subject to fluctuations in demand and price.

1.3.2 Trading Coffee as a Commodity:

The trading of coffee as a commodity is done through various exchanges, such as the Intercontinental Exchange (ICE), the New York Mercantile Exchange (NYMEX), and the London International Financial Futures and Options Exchange (LIFFE). The exchanges provide a marketplace where coffee buyers and sellers can come together and negotiate prices based on supply and demand conditions. The prices that are set on these exchanges play a major role in determining the price of coffee for consumers, as well as for farmers and other participants in the coffee industry.

1.3.3 Grading and Classification of Coffee:

When coffee is traded as a commodity, it is graded based on various factors, such as the type of bean, the size, and the color. The coffee is then categorized into different grades, with each grade having a different price based on its quality and attributes.

The most common grading systems for coffee are the Specialty Coffee Association (SCA) system. (Before 2018 these were 2 different systems SCA and SCAE and from January 2018 they merged into 1 association called SCA) and Coffee Quality Institute system (CQI)

These grading systems are designed to provide a standardized method for evaluating the quality of coffee and ensuring that coffee buyers and sellers have a common understanding of what they are buying and selling.

1.3.4 Factors that Impact the Price of Coffee

The price of coffee is influenced by several factors, including supply and demand, production costs, and currency exchange rates. Some of the key factors that impact the price of coffee include:

- Supply and demand: As with most commodities, the price of coffee is heavily influenced by supply and demand. If demand for coffee is high, prices will likely rise, and if demand is low, prices will likely fall. To meet the increasing demand for coffee, producers must expand production, which can drive up costs and impact the price of coffee.

- Production costs: The cost of producing coffee is influenced by a number of factors, including labor costs, fertilizer and pesticide costs, and transportation costs. These costs can fluctuate, impacting the overall cost of production and the price of coffee.

- Currency exchange rates: Coffee is traded globally, and fluctuations in currency exchange rates can impact the price of coffee. For example, if the value of the U.S. dollar decreases, the price of coffee traded in dollars will likely increase, as it will cost more for producers to purchase the inputs needed to produce coffee.

In conclusion, coffee as a commodity is an important aspect of the coffee industry that impacts both commercial and retail coffee businesses. Understanding the factors that influence coffee prices and quality is crucial for success in the industry. By staying up to date on coffee trends and market conditions, coffee businesses can make informed decisions about sourcing, roasting, and selling coffee. Additionally, it is important to have a deep understanding of the coffee supply chain, from farm to cup, to ensure the coffee being offered is of the highest quality and ethically sourced. With the right knowledge and strategy, coffee businesses can successfully navigate the coffee commodity market and thrive in the coffee industry.

1.4 Coffee supply chain:

The coffee supply chain refers to the journey of coffee from the time it's harvested as a crop on the farm to when it reaches the consumer as a finished product. A typical coffee supply chain involves several different players, each of which has a role in bringing the coffee from the farm to the market.

1.4.1 Coffee Producers:

Coffee producers are the farmers or growers who cultivate coffee plants. They can be individuals, families, or large corporations that own multiple farms. The size of a coffee farm can range from a few hectares to several thousand hectares.

1.4.2 Coffee Exporters:

Coffee exporters are the companies or organizations that buy coffee beans from producers and export them to coffee importers in other countries. They are responsible for handling the logistics of getting the coffee beans from the farm to the port, and then to the importer.

1.4.3 Coffee Importers:

Coffee importers are the companies or organizations that buy coffee beans from exporters and bring them into their own country. They are responsible for handling the logistics of getting the coffee beans from the port to their own warehouse, and then distributing the coffee beans to roasters.

1.4.4 Coffee Roasters:

Coffee roasters are the companies or individuals who buy green coffee beans from importers and roast them to make the coffee that we drink. They are responsible for selecting the right beans for the right roast profile, and then roasting them to bring out the desired flavors and aromas.

1.4.5 Coffee Retailers:

Coffee retailers are the companies or individuals who sell coffee to consumers. They can be coffee shops, cafes, supermarkets, or online retailers. Coffee retailers buy coffee from roasters, and then package and sell it to consumers.

1.4.6 Coffee Consumers:

Coffee consumers are the end-users of the coffee supply chain. They are the people who buy and drink coffee.

1.4.7 The Importance of Sustainable Coffee Production:

Sustainable coffee production is a critical component of the coffee supply chain. It ensures that coffee can be produced in a way that protects the environment, supports the livelihoods of coffee farmers, and guarantees a consistent supply of high-quality coffee for consumers.

Conclusion is that coffee supply chain is a complex and interconnected system that involves many different

players. Each player in the supply chain has a critical role to play in bringing coffee from the farm to the consumer. Understanding the coffee supply chain is important for anyone who is interested in the coffee industry, whether as a consumer, producer, roaster, or retailer. By understanding the coffee supply chain, we can better appreciate the journey that coffee takes from the farm to our cup, and the efforts that are made to produce high-quality coffee in a sustainable and responsible manner.

1.5 Market trends and statistics in the coffee industry:

The coffee industry is a dynamic and rapidly changing market, with new trends and developments emerging on a regular basis. In this section, we will examine some of the most recent market trends and statistics in the coffee industry to help provide a comprehensive overview of the market and its current state.

One of the most important indicators of the state of the coffee industry is its market size and growth. According to recent data, the global coffee market is expected to reach

$48.9 billion by 2025, growing at a compound annual growth rate (CAGR) of 6.2% from 2020 to 2025. This growth is driven by several factors, including increasing demand for high-quality coffee, the rise of specialty coffee shops, and the growing popularity of at-home coffee consumption.

The coffee market can be segmented into several key segments, including retail coffee, commercial coffee, and instant coffee. Within these segments, there are several sub-segments, such as specialty coffee, gourmet coffee, and decaf coffee, that are growing in popularity. Understanding the different segments of the market and their unique characteristics is important for developing effective marketing strategies and understanding the competitive landscape.

To better understand the market, it is important to also consider consumer trends and behaviors. Currently, there are several key trends shaping the coffee industry, including a focus on health and wellness, sustainability and eco-friendliness, and convenience. Consumers are increasingly looking for high-quality, healthy, and sustainable coffee options, and are willing to pay a premium for these products.

To provide a more comprehensive understanding of the coffee industry, it is also important to consider key market statistics, such as coffee consumption patterns, the popularity of different coffee types and brewing methods, and the role of coffee in the overall food and beverage market.

The coffee industry is a dynamic and rapidly growing market, with several key trends and developments shaping its current state. Understanding these trends and statistics is essential for developing effective marketing strategies and navigating the competitive landscape. By staying informed and up to date on the latest developments in the market, coffee businesses can position themselves for success and growth in the years to come.

1.6 Key players in the coffee industry:

The coffee industry is complex and encompasses many players from growers to retailers. Understanding the key players in the coffee industry is important to understand the market and competition, as well as potential suppliers and customers.

1.6.1 Coffee Growers:

Coffee growers are the primary producers of coffee. They are responsible for growing, harvesting, and processing the coffee beans. There are two main types of coffee growers: small-scale farmers and large commercial coffee estates. Small-scale farmers typically grow coffee as a subsistence crop, while large commercial coffee estates produce coffee as a commercial commodity.

1.6.2 Coffee Cooperatives:

Coffee cooperatives are organizations that bring together small-scale coffee growers in order to improve their access to markets and support the development of their businesses. By pooling their resources, coffee cooperatives can negotiate better prices for their members, provide credit and technical support, and ensure that the quality of their coffee is consistent.

1.6.3 Coffee Traders:

Coffee traders are intermediaries that purchase coffee from growers and then sell it to roasters and other buyers. They are responsible for negotiating prices, arranging transportation, and ensuring that the coffee meets the quality standards of their clients.

1.6.4 Coffee Roasters:

Coffee roasters are the companies that buy coffee from traders and then roast it to produce the final product that is sold to consumers. Roasters are responsible for determining the roasting profile for each coffee, which will affect the flavor and aroma of the final product.

1.6.5 Coffee Retailers:

Coffee retailers are the companies that sell coffee to consumers. They include specialty coffee shops, cafes, and supermarkets. Coffee retailers are responsible for sourcing coffee, brewing, and serving it, and marketing it to customers.

1.6.6 Coffee Equipment Manufacturers:

Coffee equipment manufacturers are the companies that produce the equipment used in the coffee industry, including espresso machines, grinders, and brewers. They are an important part of the supply chain, as the quality of the equipment can greatly impact the quality of the final product.

1.6.7 Specialty Coffee Associations:

Specialty coffee associations are organizations that represent the interests of the specialty coffee industry. They provide support to coffee growers, roasters, and retailers, and promote the growth and development of the specialty coffee industry.

In conclusion, the key players in the coffee industry play a critical role in the production, distribution, and sale of coffee. Understanding these players and their roles is essential to succeed in the coffee industry, whether as a grower, roaster, retailer, or other player.

1.7 Global and regional coffee markets:

The global and regional coffee markets are a crucial aspect of the coffee industry, as they play a significant role in shaping the market trends and determining the overall demand for coffee.

1.7.1 Global Coffee Market:

The global coffee market is a highly competitive and dynamic sector, with many players vying for a share of the market. The market is dominated by countries in South America and Africa, which together produce around 75% of the world's coffee. The largest coffee-producing countries are Brazil, Vietnam, Colombia, Indonesia, and Ethiopia. In terms of consumption, Europe and North America are the largest markets, with the United States alone consuming around 25% of the world's coffee.

1.7.2 Regional Coffee Markets:

Regional coffee markets refer to the markets within individual countries or regions, which are characterized by specific market trends, consumer preferences, and local regulations. Some of the largest regional coffee markets include North America, Europe, and Asia.

North America is a mature market, with a strong demand for specialty coffee and a growing interest in single-origin and sustainable coffee. Europe is a diverse market, with varying consumer preferences and tastes, but with a growing trend towards high-quality and sustainable coffee. Asia is a rapidly growing market, with a rapidly increasing demand for coffee, particularly in China and India.

1.7.3 Market Trends and Statistics:

The coffee industry is constantly evolving, and market trends and statistics provide important insights into the current state of the industry and the prospects for growth. Some of the key market trends and statistics in the coffee industry include:

- Increasing demand for specialty coffee: Specialty coffee is growing in popularity, with consumers seeking out high-quality, ethically sourced, and sustainable coffee.

- Growing interest in sustainability: Consumers are ncreasingly interested in sustainability and are looking for coffee brands that are environmentally and socially responsible.

- Rising demand for single-origin coffee: Single-origin coffee is becoming increasingly popular, as consumers look for unique and authentic coffee experiences.

- Increasing demand for coffee shops and cafes: The demand for coffee shops and cafes is growing, as consumers seek out new and unique coffee experiences.

In conclusion, the global and regional coffee markets are a dynamic and constantly evolving sector, with a range of trends and market statistics that provide important insights into the industry. Understanding these trends and statistics is essential for success in the coffee industry, as they provide valuable information for making informed business decisions.

1.8 Environmental and social factors in the coffee industry:

The coffee industry has a significant impact on the environment and local communities, both positively and negatively. On one hand, coffee production can provide economic opportunities for farmers, their families, and local communities. On the other hand, the coffee industry has been criticized for environmental degradation, exploitation of workers, and other negative social impacts. Understanding these environmental and social factors is crucial for coffee businesses to minimize negative impacts and maximize positive ones.

1.8.1 Environmental Factors:

Coffee production requires large amounts of water, fertilizer, and pesticides, which can harm the environment and surrounding communities. For example, overuse of water can deplete local water sources, leading to water scarcity for other uses, such as agriculture, drinking water, and hygiene. Similarly, the use of chemicals can pollute water sources, soil, and air, leading to negative health impacts for workers and nearby communities. The coffee industry also contributes to deforestation, as coffee farms are often established in areas with high levels of biodiversity, such as tropical forests. Deforestation can lead to soil erosion, loss of habitat, and loss of biodiversity.

To mitigate these negative impacts, coffee businesses can adopt sustainable practices, such as water conservation, the use of natural pest control methods, and reforestation. For example, some coffee farmers use drip irrigation systems, which conserve water and reduce the need for chemicals. Similarly, shade-grown coffee farms provide habitat for wildlife and help to conserve biodiversity.

1.8.2 Social Factors:

The coffee industry has been criticized for the exploitation of workers, particularly in countries where labor laws are weak or not enforced. Coffee workers are often paid low wages, work long hours, and lack access to basic social protections, such as healthcare and education. This can lead to poverty and other negative social outcomes, such as child labor, forced labor, and human trafficking.

To mitigate these negative impacts, coffee businesses can adopt ethical sourcing practices, such as fair-trade certification, which ensures that workers receive fair wages and have access to social protections. Additionally, coffee businesses can work with suppliers to improve working conditions, such as providing workers with health and safety training, and access to healthcare.

In conclusion, understanding environmental and social factors in the coffee industry is crucial for coffee businesses to minimize negative impacts and maximize positive ones. Coffee businesses can adopt sustainable practices, such as water conservation and the use of natural pest control methods, and ethical sourcing practices, such as fair-trade certification, to minimize negative impacts and maximize positive outcomes for workers and the environment.

1.9 Challenges facing the coffee industry:

The coffee industry is a complex and dynamic sector that is facing several challenges. These challenges can be divided into three main categories: economic, environmental, and social.

1.9.1 Economic Challenges:

The coffee industry is characterized by price volatility, which affects the profitability of coffee producers, traders, and roasters. Coffee prices are influenced by various factors, including global supply and demand, weather conditions, and geopolitical events.

In recent years, there have been concerns about overproduction in some coffee-growing countries, which has led to a glut of coffee on the market and a decline in prices. This has made it difficult for coffee farmers to earn a living, and many have been forced to switch to other crops or abandon their farms.

Another economic challenge facing the coffee industry is the limited investment in coffee production, which has resulted in outdated farming practices and a lack of productivity gains. This has contributed to a decline in coffee quality and yields and has also made it difficult for coffee farmers to compete with other crops.

1.9.2 Environmental Challenges:

The coffee industry is facing significant environmental challenges, including deforestation, water scarcity, and climate change. Deforestation has reduced the amount of land available for coffee production and has also contributed to habitat loss and biodiversity decline.

Water scarcity is a major concern for coffee producers, as coffee plants are highly dependent on a consistent water supply. Climate change is also affecting the coffee industry, as rising temperatures and changing precipitation patterns are altering growing conditions and reducing yields.

1.9.3 Social Challenges:

The coffee industry is facing significant social challenges, including poverty, child labor, and exploitation. Many coffee farmers are struggling to make a living and are trapped in a cycle of poverty and debt. This has led to the exploitation of workers and has contributed to the prevalence of child labor in coffee-growing regions.

In addition, coffee production often involves the use of hazardous chemicals, which can have negative impacts on the health of workers and the environment. This has raised concerns about the sustainability of coffee production and has led to calls for greater transparency and accountability in the coffee industry.

In conclusion, the coffee industry is facing significant challenges, and it is essential that these challenges are addressed in a responsible and sustainable manner. This will require the cooperation of all stakeholders, including coffee producers, traders, roasters, and consumers, to ensure the long-term viability of the coffee industry.

1.10 Opportunities in the coffee industry:

The coffee industry is constantly evolving and presents several opportunities for those looking to enter the market or expand their existing operations. Some of the key opportunities in the coffee industry include:

1.10.1 Premiumization:

The demand for premium and specialty coffee is growing globally, providing an opportunity for coffee businesses to differentiate themselves by offering high-quality, unique products.

1.10.2 Health and wellness:

Consumers are increasingly seeking out healthier options, and coffee is no exception. This presents an opportunity for coffee businesses to offer healthier coffee drinks and promote the health benefits of coffee.

1.10.3 Sustainability and ethical sourcing:

As consumers become more aware of environmental and social issues, there is growing demand for sustainably and ethically sourced coffee. This provides an opportunity for coffee businesses to differentiate themselves by offering sustainably sourced and fair-trade certified coffee.

1.10.4 Innovation:

The coffee industry is constantly innovating, with new products and technologies emerging all the time. This presents an opportunity for coffee businesses to stay ahead of the curve and offer cutting-edge products and experiences to their customers.

1.10.5 Expansion into new markets:

The global coffee market is growing, and there are opportunities for coffee businesses to expand into new markets and tap into new customer segments.

By taking advantage of these opportunities, coffee businesses can grow and succeed in a rapidly changing and highly competitive industry. To make the most of these opportunities, however, coffee businesses must be well-informed, strategic, and proactive. They must stay up to date on market trends and consumer preferences and be willing to take calculated risks and make the investments necessary to capitalize on emerging opportunities.

CHAPTER 2

MARKET RESEARCH

This chapter will focus on the importance of market research for setting up a coffee business. You will learn about the different methods for conducting market research, such as online surveys, focus groups, and market analysis. You will also learn about the key information you need to gather through market research, such as your target market, competition, and market trends.

As a coffee consulting expert, I cannot stress enough the importance of thorough market research when starting a coffee business. This research will help you understand the market demand, competition, and target audience, allowing you to make informed decisions about your business.

In this chapter, we'll go through the steps you need to take to conduct effective market research for your coffee business.

Step 1: Define your target market:

The first step in market research is to identify your target market. Who are the customers you want to serve? What are their characteristics, preferences, and behaviors? This information will help you create a profile of your ideal customer, which you can use to guide your marketing and sales efforts.

Step 2: Study your competition:

Once you've defined your target market, the next step is to analyze your competition. Who are your competitors, what do they offer, and what are their strengths and weaknesses? This information will give you a better understanding of the market and help you determine your unique selling proposition.

Step 3: Analyze the market demand:

The next step is to analyze the market demand for coffee. This can be done through surveys, focus groups, or by looking at industry data and trends. You need to understand the demand for coffee in your target market, including the types of coffee they prefer, the prices they are willing to pay, and the frequency of their purchases.

Step 4: Gather market intelligence:

Finally, it's important to gather market intelligence. This involves staying up to date with industry news, trends, and innovations, as well as monitoring consumer behavior and preferences. This information will help you stay ahead of the curve and make informed decisions about your business.Market research is an essential step in starting a coffee business, as it helps you to understand the market demand, competition, target audience, and other important aspects that can impact your business.

2.1 Understanding the Coffee Industry:

The coffee industry is one of the largest and most competitive industries in the world. It covers everything from the cultivation of coffee beans to the sale of coffee products. The industry is divided into two main categories: the coffee shop industry and the coffee roastery industry.

2.2 Conducting Market Research:

Market research is a systematic process of collecting, analyzing, and interpreting data about the market, competition, target audience, and industry trends. The goal of market research is to gather information that will help you make informed decisions about your business. There are several methods for conducting market research, including online research, surveys, focus groups, and competitor analysis.

2.3 Key Findings:

The key findings of your market research will help you to identify the opportunities and challenges that you will face as you start your coffee business. These findings will also help you to make informed decisions about your business strategy and marketing plan.

Market research is a crucial step in starting a coffee business. It provides valuable insights that will help you make informed decisions and increase your chances of success. Make sure to take the time to conduct thorough market research before starting your coffee business.

CHAPTER 3

BUSINESS PLANING

In this chapter, you will learn about the importance of creating a comprehensive business plan. You will be taken through the step-by-step process of creating a business plan, including how to conduct a SWOT analysis, how to set business goals and objectives, and how to create a financial plan.

Starting a coffee business can be an exciting and challenging venture. It's essential to have a well-defined plan in place to help guide your decision-making and ensure that your business is successful. In this chapter, we'll discuss the importance of creating a business plan and the steps involved in the process.

3.1 Importance of a Business Plan:

A business plan is a comprehensive document that outlines your business's objectives, strategies, and financial projections. It's essential to have a business plan in place before you start your coffee business. A well-defined plan can help you:

- Stay organized and focused
- Secure funding from investors or lenders
- Attract and retain customers
- Assess the potential success of your business

3.2 Steps for Creating a Business Plan:

There are several key steps involved in creating a business plan. These include:

- Defining your business vision and mission
- Conducting a SWOT analysis
- Creating a marketing plan
- Developing a financial plan

3.2.1 Defining Your Business Vision and Mission:

The first step in creating a business plan is to define your business vision and mission. Your business vision should describe your long-term goals and aspirations, while your mission statement should articulate the purpose of your business. This will help you to stay focused and motivated as you work to achieve your goals.

3.2.2 Conducting a SWOT Analysis:

SWOT Analysis is a valuable tool for evaluating a business idea, and it can be used to assess the feasibility of starting a coffee shop or roastery.

SWOT stands for Strengths, Weaknesses, Opportunities and Threats, and the goal of this analysis is to identify these key aspects of your business.

Strengths:

This section should focus on what makes your business idea unique and what advantages you have over your competitors. For example, your location, quality of coffee beans, expertise in coffee brewing, etc.

Weaknesses:

This section should focus on areas where your business may fall short. For example, lack of experience, limited marketing budget, small market share, etc.

Opportunities:

This section should focus on new or emerging trends in the coffee industry that you can take advantage of. For example, the trend towards sustainability, new marketing channels, etc.

Threats:

This section should focus on factors that could negatively impact your business, such as competition from larger coffee chains, price changes in the coffee industry, changes in consumer preferences, etc.

To conduct a SWOT analysis, first gather as much information as you can about your business idea and the coffee industry. Then, take the time to consider each of the four areas of the SWOT analysis and identify what you see as your strengths, weaknesses, opportunities, and threats.

This information will help you refine your business idea and better understand the challenges and opportunities you will face as you move forward. By completing a thorough

SWOT analysis, you will be in a much better position to make informed decisions about your business and to develop a strong business plan.

3.2.3 Creating a Marketing Plan:

Your marketing plan should outline the strategies and tactics that you will use to promote your coffee business. It should describe your target market, your marketing mix (product, price, place, promotion), and your marketing budget.

3.2.4 Developing a Financial Plan:

Your financial plan should outline your projected revenue and expenses for your coffee business. This will help you to determine the funding that you need to start your business and to assess its potential for success. When creating a financial plan, it's important to consider factors such as the cost of supplies, labor, and marketing, as well as your sales projections.

3.3 Tips for Creating a Financial Plan:

When creating a financial plan, there are several key tips that you should keep in mind:

- Forecast revenue and expenses carefully: Make sure that you have a clear understanding of your projected revenue and expenses, including the cost of supplies, labor, and marketing.

- Develop a budget: A budget will help you to track your

spending and ensure that you are staying within your means.

- Be realistic: Don't overestimate your revenue or under-estimate your expenses, as this can lead to unrealistic financial projections.

- Plan for contingencies: Make sure that you have a plan in place for unexpected expenses, such as equipment repairs or unexpected downturns in sales.

Creating a business plan is an essential step in starting a successful coffee business. By following these steps and tips, you can ensure that you have a comprehensive plan in place that will help you to achieve your goals and succeed in the competitive coffee industry.

CHAPTER 4

CHOOSING BUSINESS STRUCTURE

In this chapter, you will learn about the different types of business structures available for your coffee business, including sole proprietorship, partnership, limited liability company (LLC), corporation and free zone company (FZC).

You will also learn about the advantages and disadvantages of each structure, and how to choose the best structure for your business.

One of the most important decisions to be made when starting a business is choosing the right business structure. The type of business structure you choose will determine the legal, tax, and operational aspects of your business, as well as your personal liability and the ownership structure of your company. In this chapter, we will provide an overview of the most common business structures and outline the pros and cons of each to help you make an informed decision.

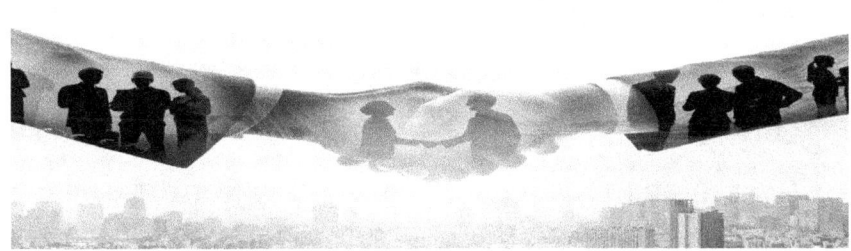

4.1 Types of Business Structures:

There are several types of business structures, each with its own legal and tax implications, as well as advantages and disadvantages. The most common business structures include:

- **Sole Proprietorship:**

  This is the simplest type of business structure and is owned and run by a single individual. A sole proprietorship is not a separate legal entity, so the owner is personally liable for all debts and obligations of the business.

- **Partnership**:

  A partnership is a business structure where two or more individuals own and run the business together. Partnerships can be general partnerships, where all partners have an equal say in the running of the business, or limited partnerships, where some partners have limited liability.

- **Limited Liability Company (LLC):**

  An LLC is a type of business structure that combines elements of partnerships and corporations. Owners of an LLC are called members and have limited liability for the debts and obligations of the business.

- **Corporation:**

  A corporation is a separate legal entity from its owners, who are known as shareholders. Shareholders elect a board of directors to manage the corporation and are not personally liable for the debts and obligations of the business.

4.2 Pros and Cons of Different Business Structures:

When choosing a business structure for your coffee business, it is important to consider the pros and cons of each. Here are some of the most common advantages and disadvantages of the different business structures:

- **Sole Proprietorship:**

  Pros include low cost and easy setup, as well as flexibility in decision making.

  Cons include unlimited personal liability and the difficulty of raising capital.

- **Partnership:**

  Pros include shared decision making and the pooling of resources, as well as the possibility of sharing liability.

  Cons include the difficulty of resolving disputes and the risk of unlimited personal liability.

- **Limited Liability Company (LLC):**

  Pros include limited liability for owners and the ability to choose the most advantageous tax structure.

  Cons include the need for formal operating agreements and potential conflicts between members.

- **Corporation:**

  Pros include limited liability for shareholders, the ability to raise capital through the sale of shares, and the potential for tax savings. Cons include the higher cost of formation and the potential for double taxation.

4.3 Factors to Consider When Choosing a Business Structure:

When choosing a business structure for your coffee business, there are several factors to consider, including:

- **Liability:**

  You should consider how much personal liability you are willing to take on for the debts and obligations of the business.

- **Taxation:**

  Different business structures have different tax implications, so it is important to consider the tax implications of each when choosing a business structure.

- **Ownership:**

  You should consider the ownership structure of your business and who will be making decisions about the running of the business.

- **Compliance:**

  Each business structure has its own compliance requirements, so it is important to consider the compliance requirements of each when choosing a business structure.

4.4 Free zone company:

FZC is a business entity that is established in a free zone or free trade zone, which is a designated geographical area within a country where certain trade and business laws differ from those in the rest of the country. These areas are designed to encourage and facilitate international trade and investment by offering a range of incentives, including tax exemptions, relaxed regulations, and simplified procedures for doing business.

Free zone companies can be structured in a variety of ways, but one common structure is the free zone company, which is a limited liability company (LLC) registered in the free zone. This type of company allows foreign individuals or companies to fully own their business in the free zone, without the need for a local partner or sponsor.

Here are some key features of a free zone company structure:

- **Ownership:**

  In a free zone company structure, foreign investors can hold 100% ownership of the business without the need for a local sponsor or partner. This gives them complete control over their business.

- **Registration:**

Free zone companies are required to register with the free zone authority, which oversees the regulation and administration of the free zone. This involves submitting the necessary documents and obtaining the necessary licenses and permits to operate.

- **Taxation:**

Free zone companies are generally exempt from local taxes, including corporate income tax, customs duties, and other taxes. This can provide significant cost savings for businesses operating in the free zone.

- **Regulations:**

Free zones often have relaxed regulations and simplified procedures for doing business, which can make it easier and faster to establish and operate a business.

- **Infrastructure:**

Free zones often provide a range of infrastructure and services to support businesses, such as office space, warehouses, logistics services, and other amenities. This can help businesses reduce their start-up costs and focus on their core operations.

- **Legal system:**

  Free zones often have their own legal systems and dispute resolution mechanisms, which can provide added protection for foreign investors.

Overall, a free zone company structure can offer several advantages for foreign investors looking to establish a business in a new market. However, it is important to carefully evaluate the specific regulations, costs, and benefits of operating in a free zone before making a decision.

Choosing the right business structure is a crucial decision that should be made early in the process of starting a coffee business. The type of business structure you choose can have a significant impact on the way your business operates, the level of personal liability you will have, and the amount of paperwork and compliance you will need to adhere to. It is important to consider your business goals, the size of your business, and your personal financial situation when making this decision.

I strongly advise you to search for business attorney or accountant to help you make the best choice for your coffee business structure.

CHAPTER 5

FINANCING OPTIONS

This chapter will provide an overview of the different financing options available for your coffee business, including bank loans, angel investors, crowdfunding, and grants. You will also learn about the eligibility criteria and the application process for each financing option.

Starting a coffee business requires significant capital investment. It is essential to understand the different financing options available to ensure that you have the resources you need to launch and grow your business. In this chapter, we'll explore the various financing options and provide tips to help you secure financing for your coffee business.

Overview of Financing Options:

There are several financing options available to entrepreneurs looking to start a coffee business. These options include loans, grants, and crowdfunding. Let's take a closer look at each of these options.

5.1.1 Loans:

Loans are one of the most common forms of financing for small businesses. They can be obtained from banks, credit unions, or alternative lenders. Loans can be secured or unsecured and can be used to finance a variety of business expenses, including equipment, inventory, and working capital.

Pros: Loans can provide a significant amount of capital to start or grow your business. They also offer a predictable and manageable payment schedule, making it easier to budget and manage cash flow.

Cons: Loans require a good credit score and often come with high interest rates, which can be expensive over time. Additionally, you may be required to provide collateral, such as personal assets, to secure the loan.

5.1.2 Grants:

Grants are another financing option for entrepreneurs starting a coffee business. They are typically provided by government agencies, non-profit organizations, or corporations and do not need to be repaid.

Pros: Grants can provide a significant amount of capital without the need for repayment. This can be an excellent option for businesses that are just starting out and do not have a proven track record of success.

Cons: Grants can be difficult to secure and often have strict eligibility requirements. Additionally, the application process can be time-consuming and competitive, with many businesses competing for a limited pool of funds.

5.1.3 Crowdfunding:

Crowdfunding involves raising capital from many individuals through the internet. It is a relatively new financing option that has become increasingly popular in recent years.

Pros: Crowdfunding allows entrepreneurs to reach a large audience and secure funding from a wide range of sources. It also provides a platform for businesses to build a following and engage with potential customers.

Cons: Crowdfunding campaigns can be time-consuming and require significant effort to promote and market. Additionally, there is no guarantee of success, and many crowdfunding campaigns fail to reach their funding goals.

5.2 Tips for Securing Financing:

Regardless of the financing option you choose, there are several steps you can take to increase your chances of securing financing for your coffee business.

- Develop a comprehensive business plan: A well-written business plan can help convince potential investors or lenders that your business is viable and worth supporting.

- Build a strong credit history: A good credit history can increase your chances of securing a loan or other form of financing. Make sure to pay your bills on time and maintain a positive credit score.

- Network and reach out to potential investors: Building relationships with potential investors can increase your chances of securing financing. Attend industry events, join business organizations, and reach out to individuals who have experience in the coffee industry.

Consider partnering with other businesses: Joining forces with other businesses in the coffee industry can increase your chances of securing financing. Look for businesses with complementary skills and expertise and consider forming a partnership or joint venture.

Choosing the right financing option for your coffee business is a critical decision that can impact the success of your business. Each financing option has its pros and cons and it's important to weigh them carefully before making a choice. It's also important to have a clear understanding of your financial needs, as well as your business plan, when seeking financing. Finally, be sure to do your due diligence and research each financing option thoroughly, seeking the advice of financial experts and legal professionals if necessary to help ensure that you make the right choice for your business.

CHAPTER 6

SETTING UP THE PHYSICAL SPACE

In this chapter, you will learn about the key factors to consider when setting up the physical space for your coffee business. You will learn about the importance of location, design, equipment, and décor. You will also learn about the legal requirements and regulations you need to consider when setting up your physical space.

Starting a coffee business requires careful planning and execution, especially when it comes to setting up the physical space. Whether you're opening a coffee shop or a coffee roastery, you need to create a welcoming environment that will attract customers and make them feel comfortable. This chapter will provide an overview of the steps you need to take to set up the physical space for your coffee business.

6.1 Overview of the Steps for Setting Up the Physical Space:

Setting up the physical space for a coffee business involves several key steps, including choosing a location, negotiating a lease, obtaining necessary permits and licenses, designing the interior, purchasing equipment, and installing utilities. Each step is important and should be approached with care and attention to detail.

6.2 Choosing a Location:

Choosing the right location for your coffee business is critical to its success. A good location should be accessible, visible, and convenient for customers. When evaluating potential locations, consider factors such as foot traffic, parking availability, local competition, and the overall demographic of the area.

Once you have selected a location, the next step is to negotiate a lease. Make sure to understand the terms and conditions of the lease, including the length of the lease, the rent, and any options for renewal. You should also review the lease agreement carefully to ensure that it includes any special provisions that you need, such as the right to make changes to the space. Obtaining the necessary permits and licenses is another important step in the process of setting up the physical space for your coffee business. Depending on your location, you may need to obtain a food service permit, a liquor license, or a building permit. Make sure to check with your local government to determine which permits and licenses you need to obtain.

6.3 Setting Up the Physical Space:

Once you have secured a location and obtained the necessary permits and licenses, it's time to focus on setting up the physical space. This involves designing the interior, purchasing equipment, and installing utilities.

Designing the interior of your coffee business is an important step in creating a welcoming and inviting environment for customers. Consider factors such as the layout, lighting, and furniture when planning the design of your space. You should also take into account any local zoning regulations or building codes that may affect the design of your space.

Purchasing equipment is another important step in setting up the physical space for your coffee business. You will need to purchase equipment such as coffee makers, grinders, refrigerators, and storage containers. When selecting equipment, consider factors such as quality, reliability, and energy efficiency.

Finally, installing utilities such as electricity, water, and internet is necessary to ensure that your coffee business runs smoothly. Make sure to obtain quotes from several contractors and compare the costs and services offered to make the best decision for your business.

6.4 Test and fine-tune:

Once you have set up the physical space for your coffee shop, it's important to test it out and make any necessary adjustments. This may include few days before opening or to have a couple of days of soft opening with shorter working time for fine-tuning of workflow, the layout, adjusting equipment settings, or rearranging furnishings. It's also important to keep the space clean and well-maintained to create a positive experience for customers.

In conclusion, setting up the physical space for a coffee business requires careful planning and attention to detail. By following the steps outlined in this chapter, you can create a welcoming and inviting environment that will attract customers and help your business succeed.

CHAPTER 7

STAFFING AND TRAINING

This chapter will focus on the importance of hiring the right staff for your coffee business. You will learn about the different roles and responsibilities of employees in a coffee business, and how to choose the best candidates for your team. You will also learn about the importance of training your staff, including how to create a training program, what to include in your training sessions, and how to measure the success of your training program. The success of any coffee business is largely dependent on the quality of its staff and their level of training. A well-trained and motivated staff can provide excellent customer service, maintain high standards for product quality, and help to build a positive reputation for the business. On the other hand, a poorly trained staff can result in poor customer experiences, negative reviews, and decreased sales. As such, it's important for coffee business owners to invest in staffing and training as part of their overall business plan.

Steps for Hiring and Training Employees:

Setting up the physical space for a coffee business involves several key steps, including choosing a location, negotiating a lease, obtaining necessary permits and licenses, designing the interior, purchasing equipment, and installing utilities. Each step is important and should be approached with care and attention to detail.

- **Recruiting and Interviewing Candidates:**

To find the best employees for your coffee business, you need to start by creating a clear job description and posting it in various places, such as online job boards, in your local community, or on social media. Once you've received applications, it's time to start the interview process. During the interview, be sure to ask questions that will give you a good understanding of each candidate's experience, skills, and suitability for the role.

- **Providing On-the-Job Training:**

Once you've hired employees, it's important to provide them with on-the-job training to ensure they are able to perform their job duties effectively. This can include training on the use of equipment, product knowledge, customer service, and other relevant skills.

Tips for Developing a Comprehensive Training Program

- **Start with a clear training plan:**

  Before you start training your employees, you need to have a clear plan in place that outlines the training objectives and the methods you'll use to achieve them.

- **Emphasize customer service:**

  Good customer service is a key part of the success of any coffee business. Make sure that your training program covers all aspects of customer service, including communication skills, problem-solving, and conflict resolution. Always remember that good customer service is evaluated form the customer point of view.

- **Infrastructure:**

  Free zones often provide a range of infrastructure and services to support businesses, such as office space, warehouses, logistics services, and other amenities. This can help businesses reduce their start-up costs and focus on their core operations.

- **Encourage hands-on training:**

  Hands-on training is a great way for employees to learn practical skills and build confidence. Consider incorporating hands-on training sessions into your training program, such as role-playing exercises and live demonstrations.

- **Foster a positive work culture:**

  A positive work culture can help to motivate employees and keep them engaged. Make sure that your training program includes elements that help to build a positive work culture, such as team-building exercises and recognition programs.

In conclusion, staffing and training are critical components of any coffee business. By following these steps and tips, you can ensure that your employees are well-equipped to provide excellent customer service, maintain high standards for product quality, and help to build a positive reputation for your business.

CHAPTER 8

MARKETING AND PROMOTION

In this chapter, you will learn about the different marketing and promotion strategies you can use to grow your coffee business. You will learn about the importance of creating a strong brand, how to use social media and email marketing, and how to host events and promotions to attract customers.

Marketing and promotion play a crucial role in the success of a coffee business. A comprehensive marketing plan and effective marketing strategies are essential for reaching potential customers, building brand awareness, and increasing sales.

8.1 Importance of Marketing and Promotion for a Coffee Business:

Good customer service is a key part of the success of any coffee business. Make sure that your training program covers all aspects of customer service, including communication skills, problem-solving, and conflict resolution. Always remember that good customer service is evaluated form the customer point of view.

8.2 Steps for Creating a Marketing Plan:

Creating a marketing plan is an important first step in the marketing and promotion process. Your marketing plan should include the following steps:

- **Defining your target market:**

  Understanding your target market is essential for developing effective marketing strategies. You need to identify who your customers are, what their needs and preferences are, and how they can benefit from your coffee business. Basically you need to crate your perfect avatar and target that profile of potential customers through the marketing campaings.

- **Determining your marketing budget:**

  Your marketing budget should be based on the amount of money you have available for marketing and promotion, and it should reflect the size and scope of your marketing goals.

- **Selecting appropriate marketing channels:**

  Selecting the right marketing channels is crucial for reaching your target market and achieving your marketing goals. Some popular marketing channels for coffee businesses include social media, email marketing, event marketing, and in-store promotions.

8.3 Tips for Developing and Implementing Effective Marketing Strategies:

Developing and implementing effective marketing strategies is key to the success of your coffee business. Some tips for developing and implementing effective marketing strategies include:

- **Social media marketing:**

  Social media is a powerful tool for reaching potential customers and building brand awareness. You can use social media platforms such as Facebook, Instagram, and Twitter to promote your coffee business, showcase your products and services, and engage with customers.

- **Email marketing:**

  Email marketing is an effective way to reach potential customers and keep them informed about your coffee business. You can use email marketing to promote your products and services, share news and updates, and offer special promotions and discounts.

- **Event marketing:**

    Event marketing is a great way to engage with customers and build brand awareness. You can host events such as coffee tastings, workshops, and charity events to connect with customers and showcase your coffee business.

In conclusion, marketing and promotion are essential components of a coffee business plan. A comprehensive marketing plan and effective marketing strategies can help you reach potential customers, build brand awareness, and increase sales. By following the steps for creating a marketing plan and implementing effective marketing strategies, you can ensure the success of your coffee business.

CHAPTER 9

CHALLENGES AND OPORTUNITIES

In this chapter, you will learn about the common challenges faced by coffee businesses and how to overcome them. You will also learn about the different opportunities for growth and expansion in the coffee industry, including how to enter new markets and how to develop new products and services.

The coffee industry, like any other industry, is not immune to challenges and obstacles. Understanding these challenges is crucial to the success of a coffee business. In this chapter, we will discuss common challenges faced by coffee businesses and ways to overcome them. We will also highlight opportunities for growth and expansion that can help coffee businesses to stay competitive and thrive in the industry.

Common Challenges:

- **Competition:**

    Competition is one of the biggest challenges faced by coffee businesses. With the increasing number of coffee shops and cafes, it can be difficult for a new business to stand out in the market. To overcome this challenge, coffee businesses need to focus on differentiation, offering unique and high-quality products, and providing excellent customer service.

- **Rising Costs:**

    The cost of coffee beans, labor, and other inputs is constantly rising. This can put pressure on coffee businesses to increase their prices, which can be difficult in a competitive market. To mitigate this challenge, coffee businesses need to focus on improving operational efficiency, reducing waste, and finding ways to lower costs.

- **Changing Consumer Preferences:**

    Consumer preferences and tastes are constantly changing, making it difficult for coffee businesses to keep up. To stay ahead of the curve, coffee businesses need to stay informed about current trends and be open to new ideas and concepts. They also need to continuously evaluate their products and offerings to ensure they are meeting the needs of their customers.

Overcoming Challenges:

- **Develop Effective Marketing Strategies:**

  A strong marketing strategy can help coffee businesses to stand out in a competitive market and attract new customers. This may include utilizing social media, email marketing, and event marketing to reach potential customers and promote their products.

- **Improve Operational Efficiency:**

  Improving operational efficiency can help coffee businesses to reduce costs and stay competitive. This may include streamlining processes, reducing waste, and utilizing technology to automate tasks.

Opportunities for Growth and Expansion:

- **Expand Product Line:**

  Offering a wider variety of products, such as specialty drinks, baked goods, and food items, can help coffee businesses to appeal to a wider range of customers and increase sales.

- **Enter New Markets:**

  Expanding into new markets, such as international markets or new geographic locations, can help coffee businesses to reach new customers and grow their business.

In conclusion, the coffee industry is faced with both challenges and opportunities for growth and expansion. By understanding these challenges and opportunities, coffee businesses can take the necessary steps to overcome the challenges and take advantage of the opportunities for growth and success.

CHAPTER 10

CONCLUSION

In this chapter, you will find a summary of the key points covered in the book. You will also learn about the importance of acting and how to turn your business plan into a reality

The coffee industry is a growing and dynamic field that offers many opportunities for entrepreneurs and business owners. Whether you are starting a coffee shop, roastery, or another type of coffee business, there are many important considerations to keep in mind. From developing a solid business plan to choosing the right financing options and setting up the physical space, every aspect of your business must be carefully planned and executed to ensure success. In this chapter, we have summarized the key takeaways from the book, including the importance of creating a business plan, choosing the right business structure, securing financing, setting up the physical space, staffing and training employees, and marketing and promoting your business. We have also discussed the challenges and opportunities faced by coffee businesses and provided tips for overcoming these challenges and taking advantage of growth opportunities.

Starting and running a successful coffee business requires careful planning, hard work, and a willingness to adapt and evolve in response to changing market conditions and to accept the risk that follows such a project.

By following slowly and carefully the best practices outlined in this book and leveraging the strengths of your team, you can build a thriving coffee business that will be a source of pride and satisfaction for years to come. By thoroughly exploring these topics, we aim to provide you with a comprehensive understanding of the coffee industry and the steps required to start and run a successful coffee business. Whether you are considering starting a coffee shop, roastery, or other type of coffee-related business, these topics provide valuable insights and practical guidance.

In conclusion, creating successful coffee business can be a rewarding and fulfillinsg experience, but it requires careful planning, strategic thinking, and hard work followed by proper investment as well. By following the steps outlined in this book, you can increase your chances of success and build a thriving coffee business. We hope that this book has been helpful to you in your journey to starting and running a successful coffee business. **GOOD LUCK!**

ABOUT THE AUTHOR

 *Dragan Ristic is a coffee expert with a wealth of experience in the hospitality industry with a focus on coffee, he has spent over almost two decades (18 years and counting) working in various roles within the hospitality industry, in a few different countries gaining a deep understanding of the nuances and complexities of the coffee markets, both commercial and specialty coffee markets.*

In addition to his practical experience, Dragan is also a certified SCA (Specialty Coffee Association) trainer and a certified Q Arabica grader.

This demonstrates his dedication to staying up to date on the latest industry trends and best practices, and his commitment to delivering high-quality products and services to customers.

Dragan is also the owner of Rista Barista Roastery, a successful coffee business that he started and has been successfully managing in the highly competitive UAE market. Despite the challenges of starting and running a business in this market, where there is probably more than 100 coffee roasteries and couple of hundreds of Specialty Coffee shops Dragan has been able to build a successful and sustainable business without any investor, completely on his own with his 18 years of practical experience

Overall, Dragan Ristic is a respected and experienced coffee expert who has a deep understanding of the coffee industry and a track record of success in the hospitality industry and as an experienced business owner and industry expert, Dragan is well-positioned to provide valuable insights and guidance to those looking to set up and run a coffee business. His unique perspective and hands-on experience make him an ideal author for a book on business setup in the coffee industry.